CW00553550

THE CHAOS

DERRON SANDY

NEW WALK EDITIONS
Nottingham & Leicester

Copyright Derron Sandy 2023

978-1-7392812-2-9

Derron Sandy has asserted his right under Section 77
of the Copyright, Designs and Patents Act 1988 to be
identified as the sole author of this work.

Published by New Walk Editions
c/o Nick Everett, Centre for New Writing,
University of Leicester, LE1 7RH
and
c/o Rory Waterman
Department of English, Linguistics and Philosophy,
Nottingham Trent University, NG11 8NS

www.newwalkmagazine.com

All rights reserved. No part of this work may be
reproduced or used in any form or by any means without
the prior written permission of the publisher.

Printed by imprintdigital, Upton Pyne, Exeter.

Contents

Ghostman's Wake

Three big stone and Ghostman's brother could make an outdoor stove
to light up a dark night in a mourning yard.
Bottle and spoon to make a riddim
with Crix, crix-pan and a goatskin drum.
Djembe man possess young hot gyal to wine low.
An older woman, jealous of the demons, gets up and bawls:
"Yuh now come out, young gyal!"

Three items: empty beer bottle, kerosene and cloth.
Flambeau lit up a dark street, a parade of masquerades.
Aged hands with curled indexes shoot rum to the floor:
"One for you, Ghostman!"
Ghostman's last girlfriend costumes her sorrow
in hot curse words and empty threats of vengeance:
"I will kill dey *mother c* - - - for you, Ghostman!"

Three men: a neighbour, Ghostman's partner and someone's boy child.
Neighbour lit up by the thought of winning the dominoes gamble.
Ghostman's partner playing dominoes too, but he mind on a crime scene,
distracted by the casual horror of Ghostman's beheading.
Neighbour take the child for granted
but boys have the same acumen as men.
"Pass my winnings, Mr Stevens," the child says.

Three warnings: stranger, unattended pot and a silent djembe.
Strangers do not pay respects to the executed,
Ghostman's brother never left his outdoor stove unattended,
djembe man stop cut drum, he say something off.
A gunshot dismantle the orchestra and flip the pot too.
Mourners meander around hot oil, except Ghostman's mother.
"They kill muh next son. All in dem *mother c* - - -!"

Gusty Exchanges with the Wind

There is one loose, rogue leaf that has no place in Mr. Sam's yard.
Not on his pristine, power-washed for Christmas concrete,
not on his unused driveway just buttered by bristles of his fex broom –
so speckless, he could put bread to toast on that sun-baked platform
that even kings would eat.

This one leaf, though, refused to be bagged;
it brags about nimbleness, says something about levitating
and banishes Sam's arthritic everything.
"But you are dried out as I am," Sam responded.
He dropped his broom and went after the leaf;
just like all his grandchildren, it was out of reach
as it signed pact with the wind to outskill
his Saturday morning ritual.
The gusts grew and the leaf thought it would never be caught.
Mr. Sam, now a hobbling statue of frustration,
watched as small whirlwinds danced on the fragments of his patience.

Last night the wind blew one of Mr. Sam's offspring
through our rickety back window my older brother refused to mend.
The younger Sam, out of wind, was trapped in the wrought-iron gate.
According to the wind of rumours, circulating from the district hospital,
the blow my father dealt him was fatal.

I wondered how such a spoilsport could grow
in a yard made so perfect each Sabbath.

To the Man who Stood Up to an Angry Man and a Cutlass

We have laughed at your bravado.
Don't you know you could dead easy here
by choking on the residue of the cuss
you coughed up on your enemy
to infect him with ills about his mother?
He vows to return,

which is a preface to your eulogy.
You must be the most avid reader
because the way you did stand up wide-eyed
had to mean that you wanted to see
even in between all three lines on the blade.
You also said, "chop me nah."

You in the hospital now
digesting the crumbs of bravado,
your face too strained to boast.
You may do well to note
that no one in the *lacaray* found you smart or brave.
Now the incident is as viral as the cuss you land on him.

Black Problems

If you born black – yuh have problems.
If you born black and poor – yuh have problems.
If you born black and poor and you living in a designated ghetto – yuh have
   problems.
If you born black and poor and you living in a designated ghetto with a single
   black mother – yuh have problems.

If you born black and poor and you living in a designated ghetto with a single
   black mother who finds hope in a black man living in the same area where
   you born – yuh have problems.

If you born black and poor and you living in a designated ghetto with a single
   black mother who finds hope in a black man living in the same area where
   you born because your father busy living in the area where you born – yuh
   have problems.

If you born black – yuh have problems.
If you born black and poor – yuh have problems.
If you born black and poor and the man your mother finds hope in, is the man
   who influencing you like a god – yuh have problems.
That man who influencing you like a god, have a village of angels just like him
and villages learn to raise children in his likeness.

The police then learn to spell your name with hell ink – problems.
The police will write your eulogy on the edge of an assault rifle – problems.
Place you in a position to say your final prayers then perform that eulogy on
   your chest according to the village of angels.

If you born black and poor and you learn to block the roads to reason – yuh
   have problems.
If you born black and poor and you learn to block the roads to reason and
   reasoning comes in the form of swearing and spreading the village's refuse
   over the government road and when police come, you refuse to move from
   the government road as you are now part of a chorus that says,

"We nuh going nowhere," in spite of brute force ——

God will relax on your prayers
and the smoke will clear
because the nation will swallow it in
and hold its breath
and choke to death
before they give you an ear
because you born black and poor and you living in a designated ghetto with
     a single black mother who finds hope in a black man living where you
     born because

your blasted father too busy living where you living,
living like everybody else.

Children will Play Rough

"We have to find Jahna, is we own fault," said Junior.
"Not me! I gone home cause mammy say that after it dark
to come back and besides she must be dead.

You shoulda never play that game,
look what the sign said,
no horseplay, no diving, no rafting, no fishing.

You horse her and dive her and raft her – now fish her.
And I sorry, Junior, but I not coming.
I dunno how to wake up someone from drowning."

And with that Janessa went home,
leaving Junior bewildered by the river alone saying:
"Lord, mammy go kill me if I lost she last daughter."

With tears in his eye he made one last call: "Jahna!!"
No one answered except the evening's last cock.
Scared as a hen, he flapped thirty feet to kiss a rock.

Maybe for luck, maybe out of fear.
Janessa met Jahna at the beginning of the trace that led to the river.
Running. Giggling. Running.

A Cashier will Kill an Employer for this Reason

The day comes when you start creating somethings out of nothings and that in itself is an intense madness. People will respond by saying "is just so it happen" and "outta the blue" and "the mad woman trip off" and other things that will ferry their ways into the inaudible realms.

In the night he used to turn a beast and she was a cave for him to rest in and one day the cave caved in and the knife that run a jagged trail from cheek to collarbone is how she excavated his demons from resting inside her. Is never just so or outta the blue or trip off. Is calculated.

Is the ability to see yourself dead from the next side of the chaos and claw your way back to life. Is stiff resistance against being twice owned (as woman and employee). Is retribution, Lucifer, for every man you hypnotise by waving his own prick in front him. Is justice.

Barrel

for Keyana Cumberbatch

Before skybox, we were barrel people.
A barrel was a big thing – a first coming
set upon a sacrifice of the lower middle class.
When mummy leaves, know a barrel coming.

Barrel people know clearing takes a day.
Customs going and comb through your things
as if to weigh the work of your migrant mother,
while you pray for low fees and patience.

The barrel used to hold life and hope
so this thing about placing bodies in them
is contrary to all things West Indian.

Dwayne, you also searched for our missing child,
as if she had an unknown visa and took flight
away from your foreign molest and murder.

Revelations

The Revelation of Jesus Christ, which God gave unto him, to shew unto his servants things which must shortly come to pass; and he sent and signified it by his angel unto his servant John:
Who bare record of the word of God, and of the testimony of Jesus Christ, and of all things that he saw.
Blessed is he that readeth, and they that hear the words of this prophecy, and keep those things which are written therein: for the time is at hand.
                                                        Revelation 1: 1—3

As a result of Revelation, prepare for war
arm yourselves with bottles and shards and sharps
like nail file and ice pick and practice quick
jabs in soft tissue areas like neck and eye
and learn a warrior cry
the one that stretches from a PH Car to your only lifeline
calculate the amount of time it takes to be drugged
stay alert
aware
in love with life with the light of the world
who tell you that the desperate ways of men cannot be killed
without the revealing of his spirit and truth
and if the best believer sees the root of evil
then tell the next feeble forum to fix an unfixable system
to kiss your unbroken hymen and find men
who pose threat and dispose of them
I bet no number of protests could baptise a man
no number of protests could baptise a man
born in sin and shapen in Andrea and Ashanti
who become verbs for battlefields
where Banfields don't stand a chance
don't even stand
tell the funders to fund arms
instead of plans to preach to the choir
tell the police to turn another blind eye
when a woman already born awry into this world
hurls her fire and makes Jesus' job a bit easier

for real ministry is separating the wheat from the tares
is making sure that a country does not weep
in the fear that their girl child coming next
God bless my daughter with a pepper step
a sniper eye and a heart unashamed
of the Gospel of Christ
to heap coals on her enemies
to keep your heart cold if it means
that you have to kill a man dead.

Because according to Revelations
blessed is she that readeth
and blessed is she that seeth
that this is the bitter acceptance of her existence —
Some men offer the devil no resistance.

Seal not the sayings of the prophecy of this book: for the time is at hand.

For Jamal

June 8, 1997

You were born.
I remember being excited for you to come home.
Not sure the reason, but excitement bled into experience.
You were my favourite baby to date
and you increased in wisdom,
if not in stature,
but your temper grew hot like melting iron.
You were designed for self-implosion.

June, 2009

You crack the top 100 in S.E.A.
Off to St. Anthony's, the first college boy.
Your temper flared to expulsion,
closing doors of potential,
fire for redemption.
This is how caskets are opened:
refuse a lifeline
for a tug of war.

January 1, 2020

You crack the first shots for the decade,
trampled police law and lawman
with brazen immortality,
then died as law stompers all do.
The only thing resembling a comet on the night of your demise
was the rapid response of reluctant police lights
in no rush to the Arima Health Care facility.
In like manner your temper faded to some sort of eternity.

January 8, 2020

A bullet wound in the left side of your forehead.
We learnt that was a temper cooler.
During your eulogy we learnt that you read Psalms 22, not 23.
I play a djembe to entertain you.
I see blood in the eyes of your friends,
not new blood though,
they are not moved by this in any new direction.
I felt a sad relief as I remembered June 8 —

Class Prefect

A standard two prospect for prefect
could perfect the prereqs of politics.

He takes a friendship with secrets in it,
dangles those secrets as bait for a vote.

Even though the opposition has no hope,
he believes in vitriol, blackmail and hostility.

If it works for the real politicians on TV
it must work here too, in this standard two.

He levelled to a friend who already believed
that he was the cure for every human being.

Now her secret ballot balloons on his whim,
her mother's drug addiction becomes a spirit

to wander from his vile lips
at any point in his campaign.

He won the election – a landslide too.
Served for one term, a badge as proof

that power will move
even a child to the brink of insanity.

Drawing the Perfect F

the chaos of penmanship as explained by a wife, whose husband, a teacher, was caught sleeping with a female student whose father was part of a violent gang

it is an oFFense by itselF without justiFication. there are two Fs in oFFense – the word itselF
is hidden penmanship classes. For those interested in drawing oFFense: stand like a vertical
line inviting yourselF as hinge For a young girl's legs to horizontally hook on. stand tall then
look down on the young lines. that will make you an F. For without these lines you are
just I, and oFFense never stands by itselF. add yourselF to the alFabet although no
spelling could strip oFF the scent that macocious neighbours said you had when
you were dragged out From the crevice of your oFFice. only your eardrums
knew consent? everything else was a marred representation of F like
a toddler
learning
to draw.
it hurts me to say this – it good for you, you rapist! another stroke to her
birth tally would have made her Eighteen! a whole diFFerent letter.
a capital E looks like an F but the F word has no E and police
could hold you For this, at least adultery is between just
you and me. i was told that you eFFed the daughter
of a G. he had a double-handle submachine gun
that holds heavy like an H, like an ache, like
her age, like a commandment.
I checked your mark book
for the child's name, she is
an A student
and A is for
attraction and
adultery and
not oFFense
but when
you stood
over those
shorter legs
the world
saw it
only
as F.

Barrel 2

on the disappearance of Kadijah Flament

To Whom It May Concern:

I wonder if you had a destination in mind,
like Caribbean parents before Aeropost and Fedex.
Or was it a spontaneous death
sprung upon a woman
who also loved the same child?

For what it is worth,
you pack the barrel
efficiently, bending the goods
to trick Customs to think
it is really less inside.

You seal it and push it in a corner
until the package burst
and start to leak out.
How many times you mop the floor
with sweetener and disinfect?

When the police came
you were naked as Eve
and you asked for a hundred years
like a new earth preparing for you
or a Satan to be bound.

Now thcrc is a motherless daughter
hoping for barrel support
and understanding from people
who know madness, chaos
and the maximum sentence.

A Dead Child

Bareback pampers dead.
Face down on concrete dead.
Four months old dead.

There is a woman
bawling for the dead
in a Trinidadian accent.

A grandmother at wits' end
dropped her grandbaby
over a ledge and the dead

child is a viral video
and a story missed
by mainstream news.

Chaos at its best.
What poem gives solace?
Not this dead one.

Mercy

And in the midst of it all
there is still reconciliation
and it beams in benevolence.

Acceptance is embarrassment.
How could someone
make sanity out of this?

Are we spoiled children?
Has our Father gone blind?
Are our misdemeanours dreams?
Who extends our time?

If the Father mad, then so is the Son.
If even after this we still live
then the real chaos is to forgive,
and restore us unto repetition.

Notes

Ghostman's Wake

The piece is partly fictional but a shooting at a wake is not unusual. I based this poem on a very specific incident occurring at the wake of a former gang member in an adjacent community. Such occasions are usually filled with rhythm.

Crix – a popular brand of crackers regularly seen at gatherings.

To the Man who Stood Up to an Angry Man and a Cutlass

lacaray – commotion and confusion.

Black Problems

'village of angels' – refers to the members of the Belmont (a suburb on the outskirts of Port-of-Spain) who protested when police fatally shot a resident in the community. The police claimed that the individual fired first while the residents claimed he was placed on his knees and executed. The residents protested by disrupting traffic flow with debris and fire. The protest spilled into the capital.

Barrel

In November 2013, Keyana Cumberbatch was reported missing from her apartment home in Maloney, a community in Trinidad. Less than a week later her body was discovered in a barrel in the same apartment. Dwayne Lewis, her stepfather, was charged for the sexual assault and murder of Keyana.

Revelations

This is naturally a performance poem. The names refer to three girls and women who have been murdered in Trinidad:

Shannon Banfield: 2016
Andrea Bharatt: 2021
Ashanti Riley: 2022

Seal not the sayings of the prophecy of this book: for the time is at hand.
Revelation 22:10.

For Jamal

Jamal was a young man filled with promise but undone by poor choices
and circumstances of lower income living. He was arrested for various
crimes and lost his life in an altercation with a member of the protective
services. To me he was like a little brother and I loved him.

S.E.A. – the Secondary Entrance Assessment to gain entry to
secondary school. Placing in the top hundred is a major
achievement.

St. Anthony's – a prestigious secondary school in Trinidad.

'comet' – c.f. "When beggars die there are no comets seen: / The heav-
ens themselves blaze forth the death of princes", *Julius Caesar* (2: ii, 31-2).

Class Prefect

Standard two in the Trinidadian education system is equivalent to Year
3 in the UK and Second Grade in the US, the year in which students are
aged 7 to 8.

Barrel 2

Kadijah Flament went missing in June 2021. For a while there were
rumours that her body was kept in a barrel at the home of a woman
who took care of Flament's child. The woman was arrested and could
be heard in the video yelling that the police should lock her up for one
hundred years. Some consider the real tragedy to be the circumstance of
Flament's daughter who lost both her biological and assumed mother.

A Dead Child

In April 2023 a viral video of a baby motionless on the ground was sent to my phone. By all accounts it seemed to be a local video.

Acknowledgements

I am nothing without God. I am not the man I am without my family. This collection started with the guidance of Arielle and Professor Funso.

Special thanks to Nick Everett and Kelsi Delaney, co-editors of the pamphlet, for their diligence.

My creative family, The 2 Cents Movement and The Quays Foundation, have given me space to exist and I am ever grateful. Finally, my friends turned family and first supporters, thank you for being there.